Freeing Your Soul

Michael J. Ramirez

Copyright © 2024 Freeing Your Soul by Michael Ramirez

All rights reserved.

No portion of this book may be reproduced without written permission from the publisher or author except as permitted by U.S. copyright law.

ISBNs:

979-8-9917027-0-6
979-8-9917027-1-3
979-8-9917027-2-0

Contents

About the Author	VII
Dedication	IX
Significance of the Word	1
The Legacy of William Tyndale and Noah Webster	3
Introduction	7
1. Understanding the Concept of Darkness in Spiritual Growth	15
2. The Power of Desire and How It Influences Our Lives	27
3. Overcoming Ignorance and Embracing Knowledge	39
4. A Zeal for Life Vs Death Wish	47
5. Kingdom of the Flesh	53
6. Foolish Wisdom vs Self	59
7. The Virtue of Forgiveness and the Consequences of Vengeance	67
8. Christ Did Not Taste Death	73
9. The Fate of the Apostles and Their Divine Mission	79
Conclusion	85
Author's Note	89
Appendix	91

About the Author

Michael J. Ramirez is a dedicated Christian, U.S. Army veteran, and passionate spiritual growth and self-improvement advocate. Born and raised in Wilmington, California, Michael grew up in a challenging environment surrounded by gang violence and poverty, experiences that shaped his resilience and faith. Despite the hardships, Michael was blessed with a close-knit community of family and friends who helped guide him through life's difficulties, teaching him the values of perseverance, faith, and service.

After serving honorably in the U.S. Army Special Operations Command as a Ranger and Green Beret, Michael deeply desired to continue serving others through his military and personal duties. His military experience, including multiple deployments to conflict zones, has given him unique insights into leadership, discipline, and the power of faith during times of adversity. Michael's notable achievements include receiving the Special Forces and Ranger tabs, reflecting his commitment to excellence and personal growth.

With a degree in Health Sciences from George Washington University and a heart for helping others, Michael has turned his focus toward spiritual and personal development, offering practical, faith-based solutions for overcoming life's obstacles. His personal journey of faith and growth serves as an inspiration to readers, reminding them that with God's guidance, they, too, can navigate life's challenges and emerge stronger.

To my commando brethren:

Your strength, courage, and unwavering commitment have not only shaped my life but have also illuminated the path toward inner resilience and spiritual growth. This journey is dedicated to all of you who strive not just to serve but to seek a deeper understanding of self, purpose, and faith.

Significance of the Word

Embark on a captivating journey through history with a brief history of the Word. Gain insight into the profound impact of William Tyndale's first English interpretation of the canonical Bible and the influential work of Merriam-Webster, the renowned lexicographer. Explore the timeless biblical quote, "In the beginning was the word," and unravel its contemporary relevance. With a focus on Tyndale's translation and the creation of the Merriam-Webster dictionary, experience a deeper understanding of the profound connection between language and divinity.

Uncover the fascinating parallels between these two visionaries and their enduring impact on the English language. Join me on a thought-provoking exploration of language, faith, and culture as we unravel the origins of the written word. Through this immersive experience, gain a newfound appreciation for the enduring power of language and its timeless influence on humanity.

As an Audible book listener, you'll be captivated by the timeless and profound Bible passages that address the world's beginning and the Word's significance. These verses, primarily found in the books of Genesis and John, offer a compelling narrative that speaks to the heart and mind.

The Beginning and Creation Genesis 1:1-3 (NIV) "In the beginning, God created the heavens and the earth. Now the earth was formless and empty, darkness was over the surface of the deep, and the Spirit of God was hovering over the waters. And God said, 'Let there be light,' and there was light."

In these verses, the Bible describes God's creation of the world. It begins with a formless, empty earth that God transforms through His Word. This act of speaking the world into existence emphasizes the power and authority of God's Word.

> The significance of the Word can be found in John 1:1-5, 14 (NIV):
> In the beginning was the Word, and the Word was with God, and the Word was God. He was with God in the beginning. Through him, all things were made; without him, nothing was made that has been made. In him was life, and that life was the light of all mankind. The light shines in the darkness, and the darkness has not overcome it.
> The Word became flesh and made his dwelling among us. We have seen his glory, the glory of the one and only Son, who came from the Father, full of grace and truth.

These passages from the Gospel of John explain the significance of the Word (Greek: Logos). John identifies the Word as both with God and being God, highlighting the divine nature and preexistence of the Word. The Word is also identified as Jesus Christ, who became flesh and lived among humanity. This underscores the central Christian belief in the incarnation—God becoming human in the person of Jesus.

The Legacy of William Tyndale and Noah Webster

When we think, our inner dialogue consists of words. Our mission is to get as close to the essence of those words as possible. To achieve this, we turn to Merriam-Webster's first editions of his pious dictionary entries and the Apostolic Bible Polyglot English (ABEn) text adopted by Tyndale House. These sources bring us near to the first English translation of the Bible, as commissioned by William Tyndale. Tyndale and Webster were motivated by a deep sense of divine inspiration, a concept they intended to convey to their readers.

Consider the riveting saga of William Tyndale, the daring English scholar who brought the Bible to the common folk in the 1500s. Born in Gloucestershire and educated at Oxford, Tyndale mastered Greek and Hebrew to unlock the Bible's secrets. He translated the New Testament into English with a rebellious spirit and a quill in hand, challenging the Church's Latin-only policy and shaking the religious establishment.

Ever the undercover scholar, Tyndale smuggled his translated scriptures back into England hidden among bales of goods. Betrayal struck him in 1535 in Antwerp; he was charged with heresy and met a fiery end at the stake. Yet, his legacy is miraculous. His groundbreaking translations laid the cornerstone for the King James Bible, revolutionizing English Christianity and literature. Tyndale's work ensured that even a plowboy could grasp the divine, transforming the sacred text into a treasure for the masses. Here's to William Tyndale, who dared to dream, defy, and democratize the Word!

Merriam-Webster's history is intertwined with a mission to create and preserve a unified American culture, strongly emphasizing Christianity. Noah Webster Jr., the dictionary's founding author, was one of America's first nationalists. He wrote his reference books to establish a single definition of American English, often at the expense of regional and cultural variations.

In the century following the Revolutionary War, Webster's American Spelling Book became so widespread in the newly formed United States that its sales were surpassed only by those of the Bible. "To diffuse uniformity and purity of language in America, to destroy provincial prejudices that originate in dialectical differences," wrote Webster in the preface of the speller, "is the most ardent wish of the author."

By capturing language not as it was written in England but as it was spoken in the U.S., Webster aimed to lay the foundation for a uniform American speech rooted in Christian values. Unlike other texts documenting existing modes of speech, he sought to elevate a new way of speaking, sometimes making the speller read more like a political treatise than a children's schoolbook.

Webster's motivations were commercial, political, and religious. He wanted to give Americans a language they could call their own, deeply influenced by his Christian faith. The spellings Webster promoted have become hallmarks of American English, including dropping the letter *u* in words like *color*, removing the k from mimic, and changing *centre* to *center*.

When Webster's Speller was first published, politicians debated eliminating

English altogether, with some advocating adopting German and others inventing a new language. Webster offered a compromise, envisioning a new, sanctified version of English for their fresh, independent identity. An avowed nationalist and born-again Christian, Webster was not an unbiased lexicographer. He envisioned the U.S. as the successor to the Roman and Greek empires and hoped its legacy would inspire a tradition of literature to surpass England's. Webster's dream of American exceptionalism underscores how making a dictionary is, by nature, political and religious, dictating how people communicate and practice their faith. His agenda was authoritarian, leading to total intolerance of difference.

Webster grew up in Hartford, Connecticut. He was an eighteen-year-old Yale student when the Revolutionary War broke out. A passionate patriot, he enlisted during his summer vacation but arrived late at the Battle of Saratoga, missing the action.

In Webster's youth, many Americans felt stronger loyalty to their states than to the federal government. In 1776, approximately two and a half million residents were spread across hundreds of miles from Georgia to Maine. Webster described the union between the states to George Washington as a cobweb. He feared dialects and languages like French and German would further divide the nation. According to Webster, national spelling reform would lay the foundation for national identity and pride rooted in Christian values. He advocated teaching a form of English familiar to most Americans, meaning his peers: Yale-educated caucasian men.

Webster hated the French and started a daily newspaper in 1793 to combat French influence in the U.S. *The American Minerva* promoted a pro-Federalist and pro-American agenda while documenting the atrocities of the Jacobins. After a tour in the South, he was horrified by the dialects, criticizing their pronunciation and schoolrooms.

By the early 1800s, public interest in his linguistic project waned, so Webster found fresh energy from a new source: God. In 1808, Webster said he spoke with God, confessing his sins and becoming a devout Calvinist and born-again Christian. This shifted his understanding of the dictionary to incorporate evangelism. He believed in the literal truth of Genesis and the Tower of Babel, thinking all humans once spoke the same language. With this conviction, he embarked on unscientific etymological investigations, finding common roots for words in languages from Asia, Africa, and Europe.

The final project, published in 1828, contained seventy thousand words, including uniquely American nouns like skunk and squash. Webster erased some radical spellings like *wimmen* for *women* and *tung* for *tongue* but kept changes like dropping *u* in words like *honor*.

Thus, Webster's dictionary, steeped in political, religious, and cultural significance, sought to define and unify American English, driven by a profound sense of divine mission. A strong appreciation for words and exploring their meaning through the most adventurous perspective of a dictionary will enable us to visualize the deeper and sometimes hidden meaning of scripture.

Introduction

Welcome to a journey of self-discovery and spiritual growth. This guide is designed to guide you toward understanding your core values, fostering a deeper connection with yourself, and aligning your life with the teachings of Christ and ancient wisdom. This wisdom is derived from the canonical biblical texts, the lost gospel of Thomas, and the lost gospel of Mary Magdalene.

Immerse yourself in the life-changing *Morning Gratitude Ritual*, designed to revolutionize your morning routine. Dedicate just five minutes each day to breathe deeply and reflect on three things you are grateful for and set the stage for a positive and fulfilling day ahead.

Embrace the concept of *Non-Judgmental Awareness* by devoting five minutes daily to mindfulness, fostering a habit of non-judgmental awareness for a more peaceful and centered mindset.

The *Self-Compassion Letter* exercise offers profound effects of self-care, requiring only ten-fifteen minutes to write a compassionate letter to yourself, providing healing and upliftment.

Integrate spirituality into your daily routine with the *Daily Spiritual Practice* section. Begin your day with *Morning Prayer and Meditation*, dedicating five to ten minutes to prayer and meditation on a scripture passage or teaching.

The *Gratitude Journal* prompts you to jot down three things you are grateful for each day, fostering a positive outlook.

Conclude your day with *Evening Reflection* and *Reflective Journaling*, spending five to ten minutes on each to introspect on your values and personal growth.

Lastly, dedicate ten minutes to *Mindfulness Meditation* each day, focusing on your breath and observing your thoughts without judgment.

By combining these practices, you can allocate thirty to forty-five minutes daily to embrace a holistic approach to self-care and personal growth and experience the profound impact of a daily gratitude and mindfulness routine.

The Gospel of Mary: Insights and Spiritual Guidance

The Gospel of Mary, part of the Gnostic texts discovered in the Nag Hammadi Library, provides profound insights into overcoming spiritual ignorance and ascending toward divine understanding. The text describes a dialogue between the risen Savior and the disciples, where Mary Magdalene comforts and guides them, revealing hidden knowledge given to her by the Savior. This revelation emphasizes the soul's journey past the four powers—darkness, desire, ignorance, and wrath—overcoming them with divine knowledge and attaining eternal rest.

The Gospel of Mary BG 7,1-19, 5

> [...] (pp. 1-6 missing) will matter then be [destroyed] or not?"
> The Savior said, "All natures, all formations, all creatures exist in and with one another, [5] and they will be resolved again into their own roots. For the nature of matter is resolved into the (roots) of

its nature alone. He who has ears to hear, let him hear."

[10] Peter said to him, "Since you have explained everything to us, tell us this also: What is the sin of the world?"

The Savior said, [11] "There is no sin, but it is you who make sin when [15] you do the things that are like the nature of adultery, which is called 'sin.' That is why the Good came into your midst, to the (essence) of every nature, in order to restore it [20] to its root."

Then he continued and said, "That is why you [become sick] and die, for[...] [8] of the one who[... He who] understands, let him understand. [Matter gave birth to] a passion that has no equal, which proceeded from (something) contrary to nature. Then there arises a disturbance in the whole body. That is why I said to you, 'Be of good courage,' and if you are discouraged (be) encouraged in the presence of the different forms [10] of nature. He who has ears to hear, let him hear."

When the blessed one had said this, he greeted them all, saying, "Peace be with you. Receive [15] my peace to yourselves. Beware that no one lead you astray, saying, 'Lo here!' or 'Lo there!' For the Son of Man is within you. Follow [20] after him! Those who seek him will find him. Go then and preach the gospel of the kingdom. Do not [9] lay down any rules beyond what appointed for you, and do not give a law like the lawgiver lest you be constrained by it." When he had said this, he departed.

But they were grieved. They wept greatly, saying, "How shall we go to the gentiles and preach the gospel of the kingdom of the Son [10] of Man? If they did not spare him, how will they spare us?"

Then Mary stood up, greeted them all, and said to her brethren, "Do not weep [15] and do not grieve nor be irresolute, for his grace will be entirely with you and will protect you. But rather let us praise his greatness, for he has [20] prepared us and made us into men." When Mary said this, she turned their hearts to the Good, and they began to discuss the words of the [Savior].

[10] Peter said to Mary, "Sister, we know that the Savior loved you more than the rest of women. Tell us the words of the Savior which you remember - which you know (but) we do not, nor have we heard them."

Mary answered and said, "What is hidden from you I will proclaim to you."

And she began to speak to them [10] these words: "I," she said, "saw the Lord in a vision and said to him, 'Lord, I saw you today in a vision.'"

He answered and said to me, "Blessed are you, that you did not waver [15] at the sight of me. For where the mind is, there is the treasure."

I said to him, "Lord, now does he who sees the vision see it (through) the soul (or) through the spirit?"

The Savior answered and [20] said. "He does not see through the soul nor through the spirit, but the mind which [is] between the two - that is[what] sees the vision and it is [...].'" (pp. 11-14 missing)

"[...] [15] it. And desire that, I did not see you descending, but now I see you ascending. Why do you lie, since you belong to [5] me?"

The soul answered and I said, "I saw you. You did not see me nor recognize me. I served you as a garment, and you did not know me."

When it had said this, it went away rejoicing [10] greatly.

Again, it came to the third power, which is called ignorance. [It (the power)] questioned the soul, saying, "Where are you going? In [15] wickedness are you bound. But you are bound; do not judge!"

And the soul said, "Why do you judge me although I have not judged? I was bound though I have not bound. I was not [20] recognized. But I have recognized that the All is being dissolved, both the earthly (things) [16] and the heavenly."

When the soul had overcome the third power, it went upwards and saw the fourth power, (which) took [5] seven forms. The first form is darkness, the second desire, the third ignorance, the fourth is the excitement of death, the fifth is the kingdom of the flesh, [10] the sixth is the foolish wisdom of flesh, the seventh is the wrathful wisdom. These are the seven [powers] of wrath.

They ask the soul, "Whence do you come, [15] slayer of men, or where are you going, conqueror of space?"

The soul answered and said, "What binds me has been slain, and what surrounds me has been overcome, and my desire [20] has been ended, and ignorance has died. In a [world] I was released [17] from a world, [and] in a type from a heavenly type, and (from) the fetter of oblivion which is transient. From this time on [5] will I attain to the rest of the time, of the season, of the aeon, in silence."

When Mary had said this, she fell silent, since it was to this point that the Savior had spoken with her. [10] But Andrew answered and said to the brethren, "Say what you (wish to) say I about what she has said. I, at least, do not believe that the Savior said this. For certainly these teachings [15] are strange ideas."

Peter answered and spoke concerning these same things. He questioned them about the Savior: "Did he really speak with a woman without our [20] knowledge (and) not openly? Are we to turn about and all listen to her? Did he prefer her to us?"

[18] Then Mary wept and said to Peter, "My brother Peter, what do you think? Do you think that I thought this up myself in my [5] heart, or that I am lying about the Savior?"

Levi answered and said to Peter, "Peter, you have always been hot-tempered. Now I see you contending against the woman like

[10] the adversaries. But if the Savior made her worthy, who are you indeed to reject her? Surely, the Savior knows her very well. That is why he loved her more [15] than us. Rather let us be ashamed and put on the perfect man and acquire him for ourselves as he commanded us, and preach the gospel, not laying down [20] any other rule or other law beyond what the Savior said."

When [19] [...] and they began to go forth [to] proclaim and to preach.

The Gospel According to Mary

In the opening chapter of this guide, titled *Darkness*, we delve into a vision described in the Gospel of Mary. The soul confronts Darkness, asserting its freedom and awareness imparted by the Savior, ultimately triumphing over the oppressive shadow and liberating itself from the ignorance of the material world. This narrative serves as a metaphor for our struggles and inner battles.

This book will guide you through various exercises and reflections to help you identify and embrace your values, fostering personal growth and spiritual fulfillment. Through prayer, scripture reading, and engaging with a supportive community, you will gain clarity and strength to overcome your desires and addictions. Each chapter will build upon the last, leading you toward a deeper understanding of yourself and your spiritual journey.

By recognizing and nurturing your core values, you can transform your life and align it with divine purpose. As you progress, remember that the journey of self-healing and self-improvement is ongoing, and every step you take brings you closer to true freedom and fulfillment. Let this guide be your companion on this transformative path, guiding you toward a life of purpose, integrity, and spiritual enlightenment.

Embrace the light of Christ and the wisdom of the Gospel of Mary to illuminate your path. Through self-awareness, introspection, and nurturing your core values, you will find the strength to overcome life's challenges and achieve inner peace and divine connection. Welcome to your journey of self-discovery and spiritual growth.

Chapter One

Understanding the Concept of Darkness in Spiritual Growth

Paul explained in Ephesians 6: 12-17 The Armor of God:

> [10] Finally, be strong in the Lord and in his mighty power. [11] Put on the full armor of God, so that you can take your stand against the devil's schemes. [12] For our struggle is not against flesh and blood, but against the rulers, against the authorities, against the powers of this dark world and against the spiritual forces of evil in the heavenly realms. [13] Therefore put on the full armor of God, so that when the day of evil comes, you may be able to stand your ground, and after you have done everything, to stand. [14] Stand firm then, with the belt of truth buckled around your waist, with the breastplate of righteousness in place, [15] and with your feet fitted with the readiness that comes from the gospel of peace. [16] In addition to all this, take up the shield of faith, with which you can

extinguish all the flaming arrows of the evil one. ¹⁷ Take the helmet of salvation and the sword of the Spirit, which is the word of God.

This passage can also mean that your struggle is not against flesh and blood but against the forces that govern this age's darkness. To stand firm against these challenges, we must arm ourselves with truth and righteousness, embodying the divine protection that guides us toward justice and integrity. Our struggle can be misguided if we fight against one another rather than against the true forces of darkness. To resist these temptations, we must equip ourselves with forgiveness and compassion, shielding ourselves with the virtues that foster reconciliation and harmony.

In Romans 13 11-14, Paul explains The Day Is Near:

> ¹¹ And do this, understanding the present time: The hour has already come for you to wake up from your slumber, because our salvation is nearer now than when we first believed. ¹² The night is nearly over; the day is almost here. So *let us put aside the deeds of darkness and put on the armor of light*. ¹³ Let us behave decently, as in the daytime, not in carousing and drunkenness, not in sexual immorality and debauchery, not in dissension and jealousy. ¹⁴ Rather, clothe yourselves with the Lord Jesus Christ, and do not think about how to gratify the *desires of the flesh*.

In the opening chapter titled *Darkness*, we delve into a profound vision described in the Gospel of Mary, where the ascent of the soul beyond the dominion of the seven heavenly rulers is recounted. The narrative unfolds with Darkness confronting the soul, declaring, "Halt, transgressor!" Yet, the soul, undeterred, questions its alleged transgression. Darkness retorts, asserting its realm as one devoid of enlightenment, where the illumination of knowledge is forbidden. In defiance, the soul proclaims its awareness of Darkness's deceit, a revelation imparted by the Savior, and thus triumphs over the oppressive shadow, liberated from the ignorance of the material world.

How, then, do we vanquish darkness? It is not through contemplation of darkness itself but rather through the embodiment of its antithesis within our hearts—gratitude. Consider the statistics: our world witnesses 166,859 departures (deaths) daily and 368,144 new beginnings. One need not be a Tibetan warrior-monk to express morning gratitude for the gift of life and the opportunity to embrace our core values—faith, family, and love. Each day presents a chance to draw nearer to these principles. Moreover, it invites us to savor life anew, indulging in the richness of music, the arts, tactile pleasures, and the vibrant tapestry of global cultures and their culinary and artistic expressions.

Love and light would be the opposite of Darkness. Nurture the virtuous wolf within. As good trees yield bountiful fruit, so too are we, cloaked in the redemptive grace of Christ, called to be luminaries in a world shrouded in night. We traverse the darkness, yet we are guided by light, not succumbing to the slumber of obscurity. The Almighty respects our autonomy, as exemplified by Moses's leadership and the empowerment of women.

Should one believe in the inevitability of one's choices, they fall prey to the adversary, mistaking divine will for preordained misdeeds. A pure heart and a fortified mind are our bulwarks against such deception. Vigilantly guard your heart, for it is the wellspring of life and the source of all that is good. Be sure to walk with love in your heart.

The Word "Love"

Webster defines Love, v.: In a general sense, to be pleased with; to regard with affection, on account of some qualities which excite pleasing sensations or desire of gratification.

We love a friend on account of some qualities which give us pleasure in his society. We love a man who has done us a favor, in which case gratitude enters into the composition of our affection. We love our parents and children because of their connection with us and the many qualities that please us. We love to retire to a cool shade in summer. We love a warm room in winter. We love to hear an eloquent advocate. The Christian loves his Bible. In short, we love whatever gives us pleasure and delight, whether animal or intellectual. If our hearts are right, we love God above all things as the sum of all excellence and all the attributes that can communicate happiness to intelligent beings. In other words, the Christian loves God with the love of complacency in his attributes, benevolence toward the interests of his kingdom, and the love of gratitude for favors received.

Thou shalt love the Lord thy God will all thy heart, and with all thy soul, and with all thy mind- Thou shalt love thy neighbor as thyself. Matt. Xxii.

To have benevolence or goodwill for. John iii.

The fruits of righteousness stem from acts of goodness. In nurturing these seeds on earth, we lay the foundations for an eternal harvest in the heavens.

John 15:1–27 reminds us that we are branches of the true vine, tended by the divine vinedresser. Only through unity with the vine can we bear fruit; apart from it, we are barren. False prophets, clad in the guise of innocence yet harboring malice, are discerned by the fruits they bear—just as grapes are not plucked from thorns nor figs from thistles. Every tree is known by its fruit; the good tree bears wholesome fruit, while the corrupt tree yields none. Thus, every tree that fails to bear good fruit is destined for the flames. So spread love.

As Matthew 4:16 proclaims:

> Those who dwelled in darkness have witnessed a great light; upon those in the shadow of death, a radiant light has dawned. Let us, therefore, be the bearers of this light, illuminating the path for others to follow.

It is worth exploring what grounding, amygdala hijack, window of tolerance, and emotional triggers are. This exploration will help us navigate any emotional turmoil and pave the way for this book of self-discovery and healing. It provides a practical way of dealing with life's stressors and may rid our minds of unnecessary darkness from wrongful thinking. Essentially, it is a way to identify and interrupt wrongful or harmful thinking and energy.

Grounding

Grounding is a set of simple strategies designed to help individuals detach from emotional pain such as drug cravings, self-harm impulses, anger, or sadness. It involves focusing outward on the external world rather than inward on the self, which helps bring you back to the present moment and reality.

When you're overwhelmed with emotional pain, grounding techniques provide a way to regain control over your feelings and maintain safety. By anchoring yourself to the present, you can create a healthy distance from intense emotions and prevent harmful actions. Grounding can be done anytime, anywhere, and often goes unnoticed by others, making it a discreet and effective tool for emotional regulation. Finding three seconds of grounding may aid us in avoiding an amygdala hijack and allow our hippocampus to autoregulate.

An amygdala hijack occurs when the brain's amygdala, responsible for emotional processing, reacts to stress by overriding the frontal lobes, which control rational thinking. This response is part of the fight-or-flight mechanism, originally intended to protect us from immediate physical threats. However, in modern life, it can be triggered by emotions like fear, anger, or stress, leading to sudden, irrational reactions.

Recognizing an amygdala hijack involves noticing symptoms like a rapid heartbeat, sweaty palms, and a rush of adrenaline. To counteract this, one can practice mindfulness techniques such as deep breathing to calm the mind and regain rational control. It takes several seconds to recover from an amygdala hijack, and if we do not learn to control these hijacks, the often result is guilt, shame, and strained relationships. This may include examples of plate throwing, wall punching, and using words that hurt the ones we love. Substance abuse and prenatal trauma may also contribute to a smaller hippocampus (regulates the amygdala) and exacerbate our window of tolerance.

The *window of tolerance* is a concept that describes the optimal zone of arousal in which a person can function effectively and manage emotions. Within this window, individuals can handle stress, process information, and respond to the demands of everyday life without becoming overwhelmed. When outside this window, people may experience hyperarousal (anxiety, panic) or hypo-arousal (numbness, depression).

Understanding and expanding your window of tolerance can help improve emotional regulation and resilience. Techniques such as mindfulness, grounding exercises, and self-care practices can support staying within this optimal zone.

Ten Practical and Powerful Grounding Techniques Against Darkness

- **Deep Breathing**: Take slow, deep breaths, focusing on the sensation of air filling your lungs and then slowly exhaling.

- **Physical Sensation**: Hold onto a cold object, like an ice cube, or run your hands under warm water to shift your focus.

- **Sensory Awareness**: Describe your surroundings in detail, naming objects, colors, and sounds to ground yourself in the present.

- **Counting**: Count backward from one hundred in sevens or count the number of items of a particular color in the room.

- **Movement**: Engage in light physical activity such as stretching, walking, or dancing to help reconnect with your body.

- **Touch**: Use a stress ball or a piece of fabric with a distinct texture to redirect your focus to tactile sensations.

- **Visualization**: Picture a safe, calming place in your mind, and imagine yourself there, engaging all your senses.

- **Affirmations**: Repeat calming and positive statements to yourself, such as "I am safe" or "This feeling will pass."

- **Engage Senses**: Smell something soothing like lavender, taste a strong mint, or listen to calming music.

- **Grounding Statements**: Remind yourself of the present moment by stating your name, location, and date.

These grounding techniques can help you stay connected to the present, manage overwhelming emotions, and navigate through stressful situations effectively. Recall that not one size fits all. Understanding your triggers and how to ground effectively after an internal or external trigger takes trial and error. Now that we have effective grounding techniques, let's continue with a few exercises.

Exercises

Exercise 1: Morning Gratitude Ritual

Objective: To start the day with a positive mindset by expressing gratitude.

Instructions:

- Upon waking up, take a few moments to breathe deeply and reflect.

- Think of three things you are grateful for. These can be simple, such as the warmth of your bed, a loved one, or the opportunity to experience a new day.

- Speak these gratitude's out loud or write them down in a journal.

Reflection: Notice how this practice influences your mood and thoughts throughout the day. Does starting with gratitude change how you approach challenges?

Exercise 2: Transforming Thoughts into Positive Behavior

Objective: To understand and redirect thoughts to foster positive emotions and behaviors.

Instructions:

- Identify a recurring negative thought you have during the day. For example, "I'm not good enough."

- Challenge this thought by asking yourself, "Is this true? What evidence do I have against this thought?"

- Replace negative thoughts with positive affirmations such as "I am capable and strong."

- Visualize yourself succeeding in a task or receiving praise. Imagine the emotions and behaviors associated with this success.

Reflection: Track your progress over a week. How often were you able to catch and replace negative thoughts? What changes did you notice in your emotions and behaviors?

Exercise 3: Exploring Your Thinking Style

Objective: To understand and leverage your dominant thinking style for personal growth.

Instructions:

- Reflect on how you typically solve problems or process information.

- Do you visualize, use words, or a combination of both?

Complete The Following Self-assessment:

- Do I see images in my mind when I think about something? Do I talk to myself in my mind to solve problems?

- Do I need to write things down or draw them out to understand them better?

- Based on your answers, identify if you are a visual or verbal thinker or a combination of both.

Reflection: How can you use this knowledge to improve your learning and problem-solving skills? For example, if you are a visual thinker, try using more diagrams and visual aids in your daily tasks.

Exercise 4: Cultivating a PureHeart and Mind

Objective: To develop emotional resilience and a positive outlook.

Instructions:

- Practice mindfulness meditation for ten minutes each day.

- Focus on your breath and observe your thoughts without judgment.

- When negative thoughts arise, acknowledge them, then gently bring your focus back to your breath or a positive mantra, such as "I am at peace."

- Throughout the day, take moments to check in with your heart. Are you holding onto any negative emotions? If so, practice letting them go and replacing them with feelings of love and compassion.

Reflection: Keep a journal of your meditation experiences and emotional states. Over time, observe any patterns and progress in maintaining a pure heart and mind.

Exercise 5: Aligning Actions with Core Values

Objective: To ensure your daily actions reflect your deepest values.

Instructions:

- List your top five personal values. These could include honesty, kindness, family, faith, or other important principles.

- For each value, write down one action you can take this week that embodies that value.

- At the end of the week, reflect on these actions.

- How did living in alignment with your values affect your sense of fulfillment and well-being?

Reflection: How did aligning your actions with your values influence your daily decisions and interactions? Share your experiences with a friend or in a journal.

Chapter Two

The Power of Desire and How It Influences Our Lives

James 1:12 explains how God will never <u>tempt</u> us, but he will <u>test</u> us:

> ¹² Blessed is the one who perseveres under trial because, having stood the test, that person will receive the crown of life that the Lord has promised to those who love him.
> ¹³ When tempted, no one should say, "God is tempting me." For God cannot be tempted by evil, nor does he tempt anyone; ¹⁴ but each person is tempted when they are dragged away by their own evil desire and enticed. ¹⁵ Then, after desire has conceived, it gives birth to sin; and sin, when it is full-grown, gives birth to death.

It is natural to experience hunger, sexual cravings, and the money you gain from work to buy groceries. It is a sin when this grows into gluttony, lust, and greed.

In Matthew 4 1-17, we learn how Jesus Is Tested in the Wilderness by Satan:

⁴ Then Jesus was led by the Spirit into the wilderness to be tempted [a] by the devil. ² After fasting forty days and forty nights, he was hungry. ³ The tempter came to him and said, "If you are the Son of God, tell these stones to become bread."

⁴ Jesus answered, "It is written: 'Man shall not live on bread alone, but on every word that comes from the mouth of God.'[b]"

⁵ Then the devil took him to the holy city and had him stand on the highest point of the temple.

⁶ "If you are the Son of God," he said, "throw yourself down. For it is written: "'He will command his angels concerning you, and they will lift you up in their hands, so that you will not strike your foot against a stone.'[c]"

⁷ Jesus answered him, "It is also written: 'Do not put the Lord your God to the test.'[d]"

⁸ Again, the devil took him to a very high mountain and showed him all the kingdoms of the world and their splendor. ⁹ "All this I will give you," he said, "if you will bow down and worship me."

¹⁰ Jesus said to him, "Away from me, Satan! For it is written: 'Worship the Lord your God, and serve him only.'[e]"

¹¹ Then the devil left him, and angels came and attended him.

Romans 5 is the fifth chapter of the Epistle to the Romans in the New Testament of the Christian Bible. It is authored by Paul the Apostle, who was in Corinth in the mid-50s AD. In Romans 5, we see that when we are placed through trials and tribulations, we should find peace and hope in God throughout our testing and suffering:

¹ Therefore, since we have been justified through faith, we have

peace with God through our Lord Jesus Christ, [2] through whom we have gained access by faith into this grace in which we now stand. And we boast in the hope of the glory of God.[3] Not only so, but we also glory in our sufferings because we know that suffering produces perseverance; [4] perseverance, character; and character, hope. [5] And hope does not put us to shame because God's love has been poured out into our hearts through the Holy Spirit, who has been given to us.

Further, when we look at how to control our sins and temptations, Thomas records how Jesus stated how to tame our desires before they mature into sin.

The Gospel of Didymos Judas Thomas verse 7 states:

> Jesus said, "Blessed is the lion becomes man when consumed by man; and cursed is the man whom the lion consumes, and the lion becomes man."

This quote is often interpreted as a metaphorical statement about transformation and assimilation. The idea is that when a lion is consumed by a man, it is a positive transformation. Conversely, if a man is consumed by the lion (or overwhelmed by his base instincts), it is negative, as the man loses his humanity. It's a saying that encourages mastery over one's primal instincts and the elevation of the human spirit.

Let's examine how Merriam-Webster defines sin in noun form:

> SIN, n. 1. The voluntary departure of a moral agent from a known rule or rectitude or duty, prescribed by God: any voluntary

transgression to the divine law or violation of a divine command; a wicked act; iniquity. Sin is either a positive act in which a known divine law is violated, or it is the voluntary neglect to obey a positive divine command, or a rule of duty clearly implied in such command. Sin comprehends not actions only, but neglect of known duty, all evil thoughts, purposes, words, desires, whatever is contrary to God's commands or law. 1 John iii. Matt. xv. James iv. Sinners neither enjoy the pleasures of sin, nor peace of piety. [...] Rob Hall.

Among divines, sin is original or actual. *Actual sin*, defined above, is the act of a moral agent in violating a known rule of duty. *Original sin*, as generally understood, is native depravity of heart, want of conformity of heart to the divine will, corruption of nature, or deterioration of the moral character of man, which is supposed to be the effect of Adam's apostasy and manifests itself in moral agents by positive acts of disobedience to the divine will, or by the voluntary neglect to comply with the express commands of God, which require that we should love God with all the heart and soul and strength and mind, and our neighbor as ourselves. This native depravity or alienation from affections from God and his law is supposed to be what the apostle calls the *carnal mind* or *mindedness*, which is enmity against God and is, therefore, denominated *sin* or *sinfulness*. *Unpardonable sin*, or blasphemy against the Holy Spirit, is supposed to be a malicious and obstinate rejection of Christ and the gospel plan of salvation or a contemptuous resistance made to the influences and convictions of the Holy Spirit. Matt. xii.

2. A sin-offering: an offering made to atone for sin. He hath made him to be sin for us, who knew no sin.

2 Cor. v. Sin in the verb form is:

> SIN v. 1. To depart voluntarily from the path of duty prescribed by God to man; to violate the divine law in any particular, by actual transgression or by the neglect or non-observance of its injunctions; to violate any known rule of duty. All have sinned and come short of the glory of God. Rom. iii.

Now that we have a definition for sin, let's look at the Gospel of Mary, Levi retorts to Peter, stating:

> But if the Savior made her worthy, who are you indeed to reject her? Surely, the Savior knows her very well. That is why he loved her more [15] than us. Rather, let us be ashamed and put on the perfect man and acquire him for ourselves as he commanded us, and preach the gospel, not laying down [20] any other rule or other law beyond what the Savior said.

It is similar to the Teachings of Christ as explained by the apostle Paul in Ephesians 4:22-24 in his instructions for Christian living and putting on the perfect man:

> [17] So I tell you this, and insist on it in the Lord, that you must no longer live as the Gentiles do, in the futility of their thinking. [18] They are darkened in their understanding and separated from the life of God because of the ignorance that is in them due to the hardening of their hearts. [19] Having lost all sensitivity, they have

given themselves over to sensuality so as to indulge in every kind of impurity, and they are full of greed.

20 That, however, is not the way of life you learned 21 when you heard about Christ and were taught in him in accordance with the truth that is in Jesus. 22 You were taught, with regard to your former way of life, to *put off your old self, which is being corrupted by its deceitful desires; 23 to be made new in the attitude of your minds; 24 and to put on the new self, created to be like God in true righteousness and holiness.*

This is also mirrored in the Apostle Paul's teachings of Christ in his letter to the Colossians chapter 3 5-12:

5 Put to death, therefore, whatever belongs to your earthly nature: sexual immorality, impurity, lust, evil desires, and greed, which is idolatry. 6 Because of these, the wrath of God is coming.[b] 7 You used to walk in these ways, in the life you once lived. 8 But now you must also rid yourselves of all such things as these: anger, rage, malice, slander, and filthy language from your lips. 9 Do not lie to each other, since you have taken off your old self with its practices 10 and have put on the new self, which is being renewed in knowledge in the image of its Creator. 11 Here there is no Gentile or Jew, circumcised or uncircumcised, barbarian, Scythian, slave or free, but Christ is all and is in all.

12 Therefore, as God's chosen people, holy and dearly loved, clothe yourselves with compassion, kindness, humility, gentleness, and patience. 13 Bear with each other and forgive one another if any of you has a grievance against someone. Forgive as the Lord forgave you. 14 And over all these virtues put on love, which binds them all

together in perfect unity.

Lastly, in James chapter 1 2-8, we learn about trials and temptations and that God will test us:

> [2] Consider it pure joy, my brothers and sisters, [a] whenever you face trials of many kinds, [3] because you know that the testing of your faith produces perseverance. [4] Let perseverance finish its work so that you may be mature and complete, not lacking anything. [5] If any of you lacks wisdom, you should ask God, who gives generously to all without finding fault, and it will be given to you. [6] But when you ask, you must believe and not doubt, because the one who doubts is like a wave of the sea, blown and tossed by the wind. [7] That person should not expect to receive anything from the Lord. [8] Such a person is double-minded and unstable in all they do.

In the realm of mental discipline and flow, it is said that those who cannot master their cravings for food or alcohol or are incessantly consumed by sexual thoughts are not truly free. Their psychic energy remains ensnared by these desires.

To liberate oneself, one must purge envy and greed from the heart. While sex is a natural part of life, adultery disrupts the balance. Sin is merely an act—a condition that thrives given the right environment. To avoid the pitfalls of shame and guilt, one must face their inner 'lion'—the embodiment of their vices—and either conquer it or be devoured by it. This internal struggle begins in the heart, highlighting the importance of a divine connection. Reflect upon your life and discern if any of the seven deadly sins hold sway over you. Remember, Jesus is the path, the truth, and the life. Deception leads us astray, but we can seek divine clarity through prayer.

Unchecked desire morphs into obsession, an idol that rivals our devotion to God. Idols must be vanquished, for they usurp the love meant for the Divine. Cast down these false idols from the high places of your heart. Envy and greed are also byproducts of unhealthy desires.

Consider Mary Magdalene's vision of the soul's encounter with the Archon of Desire, as told in the Lost Gospel of Mary. The Archon attempts to ensnare the soul with earthly pleasures, yet the soul declares its celestial origin and intent to return to the divine realm. Despite Archon's claim, the soul asserts its freedom, revealing that it is seen only in the flesh, not in spirit, and thus escapes with joy. This narrative mirrors our battles with addiction. Whether it be to sex, alcohol, drugs, or gambling, succumbing to these 'lions' leads to enslavement. The term 'addictus' once referred to a debtor bound to servitude; similarly, addiction binds us, preventing our ascent to enlightenment.

Challenge yourself to control these 'lions' for a day and witness the clarity that follows.

Desires can become barriers to our spiritual freedom and personal growth. Through a series of self-healing and self-improvement exercises, you'll learn to confront and manage your cravings, fostering a deeper connection with yourself and the divine.

Remember, the antithesis of addiction is not sobriety—it is connection.

Exercises

Exercise 1: Identifying Your Desires and Addictions

Objective: Recognize and acknowledge the desires that have a strong hold over your life.

Instructions:

- **Find a Quiet Space:** Sit comfortably in a quiet place where you won't be disturbed.

- **Reflect:** Think about the different desires and addictions in your life—excessive food, alcohol, sex, or any other cravings.

- **List Them:** Write down these desires in a journal. Be honest and thorough.

- **Impact Analysis:** Next to each desire, note how it affects your daily life, relationships, and overall well-being.

- **Affirmation:** End this exercise with an affirmation: "I am aware of my desires and their impact on my life. I am taking steps to understand and manage them."

Exercise 2: Purging Envy and Greed

Objective: Develop a mindset free from envy and greed, fostering a heart of gratitude and contentment.

Instructions:

- **Gratitude Journal:** Start a gratitude journal. Each day, write down three things you are grateful for.

- **Mindful Meditation:** Spend 10 minutes each day meditating on the positive aspects of your life. Focus on your breath and let go of any feelings of envy or greed.

- **Acts of Kindness:** Perform one act of kindness each day without expecting anything in return. This could be as simple as a compliment or as significant as volunteering.

- **Reflect and Connect:** Reflect on these actions in your journal. How do they make you feel? Do you notice a decrease in feelings of envy and greed?

Exercise 3: Facing Your Inner 'Lion'

Objective: Confront and manage the vices and cravings that dominate your life.

Instructions:

- **Visualization:** Visualize your desire as a lion. How does it look? How does it behave?

- **Dialogue:** Imagine having a conversation with this lion. Ask why it has such a strong hold on you and what it needs.

- **Empowerment:** Visualize yourself taming the lion. Use positive affirmations like, "I am stronger than my desires" or "I control my cravings."

- **Action Plan:** Create an action plan to manage your cravings. This could include setting boundaries, seeking support from friends or professionals, and engaging in healthy activities.

- **Review:** Regularly review and adjust your plan as needed.

Exercise 4: Seeking Divine Connection

Objective: Strengthen your spiritual connection to gain clarity and guidance.

Instructions:

- **Daily Prayer:** Dedicate time each day for prayer or spiritual reflection. Seek guidance and strength to overcome your desires.

- **Scripture Reading:** Read and reflect on scriptures or spiritual texts that inspire you. For example, reflect on the message from the Lost Gospel of Mary about the soul's declaration of freedom.

- **Spiritual Community:** Engage with a community that supports your spiritual journey. This could be a church group, meditation circle, or online community.

- **Journaling:** Write about your spiritual experiences and insights. How do they help you manage your desires and addictions?

Exercise 5: Replacing Addiction with Connection

Objective: Transform the energy used in addiction toward building meaningful connections.

Instructions:

- **Identify Relationships:** List important people with whom you want to strengthen your connection.

- **Daily Connection:** Make a conscious effort to connect with at least one person each day. This can be through a phone call, meeting in person, or writing a heartfelt message.

- **Active Listening:** Practice active listening when interacting with others. Show genuine interest and empathy.

- **Community Service:** Participate in community service or group activities that align with your interests and values.

- **Reflect:** Reflect on how these connections make you feel. Notice any changes in your cravings or desires as your connections grow.

Desire is a powerful force, but it doesn't have to control you. Through these exercises, you can transform your cravings into opportunities for growth and connection. Remember, the journey of self-healing and self-improvement is ongoing, and every step you take brings you closer to true freedom and fulfillment.

Chapter Three

Overcoming Ignorance and Embracing Knowledge

In Chapter 3, we delve into the concept of ignorance and how it impacts our emotional well-being. Ignorance can cloud our minds, fuel negative self-perceptions, and hinder our personal growth. This chapter will explore techniques from Dialectical Behavior Therapy (DBT), mindfulness practices, and strategies to overcome ignorance.

Let us approach judgment with kindness, seeking the inherent goodness in all. Through righteousness and truth, we test the spirit, discerning the true nature of others by the fruits they bear. Our goal is to illuminate facts, not to cast shadows.

Embrace a wider window of tolerance, reserving anger for moments that truly warrant it (righteous anger). If forgiveness is universal, we must stand firm against those who inflict harm upon the faithful.

Marcus Aurelius reminds us that our disturbance comes not from external things but from our own judgment of them—a judgment within our power to erase.

As defined by Merriam-Webster, pain ranges from mild discomfort to severe agony, often resulting from physical causes. Yet, we must also consider the 'inflammation' and 'derangement' of the mind—emotional pains that can be just as debilitating.

Unresolved judgments lead to a physiological response—a surge of cortisol that wreaks havoc on our bodies. The Four Agreements liken unresolved anger to drinking poison and expecting another to suffer. Forgiveness, therefore, is a gift we give ourselves, independent of reconciliation with the one who wronged us. Faith as small as a mustard seed can move mountains, but first, we must harbor forgiveness in our hearts.

The Book of Mary eloquently portrays the soul's ascent and triumph over ignorance. Confronted by the formidable force of Ignorance, the soul boldly asserts its freedom and acknowledges the perpetual transformation of earthly and heavenly realms. By emphasizing the significance of transcending ignorance, the text encourages individuals to self-reflect, extracting valuable insights from their experiences to cultivate a deeper understanding of life and personal values. This practice fosters a mindset of continual growth and enlightenment, empowering individuals to embrace knowledge and overcome ignorance actively.

Merriam defines 'judge' as the act of comparing facts or ideas to discern truth from falsehood. The Bible, too, encourages us to bring facts into the light yet cautions against condemnation.

In prayer, we find solace and truth. Sometimes, our prayers echo King David's Psalms, seeking divine intervention rather than passing judgment ourselves, "Dear Lord, you are the righteous judge; deliver me from my persecutors," we pray.

Understanding Judgment and Ignorance

Let us approach judgment with kindness, seeking the inherent goodness in all. Marcus Aurelius reminds us that our disturbance comes not from external things but from our own judgment of them—a judgment within our power to erase. Through righteousness and truth, we test the spirit, discerning the true nature of others by the fruits they bear. Our goal is to illuminate facts, not to cast shadows.

Negative self-judgment can have a detrimental impact on our well-being and personal growth. The feelings of shame and guilt that accompany self-criticism can be powerful obstacles to self-improvement. It is essential to recognize and understand the tactics of these emotions. Shame convinces us that we are fundamentally flawed, while guilt centers on our actions, implying that we have committed wrongdoing. By acknowledging these tactics, we can begin to challenge and overcome the destructive influence of negative self-judgment, paving the way for greater self-compassion and personal development.

It is essential to practice self-compassion actively to overcome feelings of shame and guilt. Treating ourselves with the same kindness and understanding that we would extend to a friend can help counteract the damaging effects of self-judgment.

Additionally, reframing negative thoughts is a powerful tool in combating these emotions. Rather than labeling ourselves as failures, we can reframe our thoughts by acknowledging mistakes as opportunities for learning and growth. By incorporating these strategies into our daily lives, we can effectively combat shame and guilt, fostering a mindset of self-compassion and personal empowerment.

Dialectical Behavior Therapy (DBT) provides valuable techniques for coping with emotional distress and enhancing interpersonal connections. A fundamental component of DBT is Open Mind Thinking, which urges individuals to adopt diverse viewpoints and minimize emotional impulsivity. Engaging in specific exercises can be beneficial for cultivating an open mind.

Exercises

Exercise 1: Perspective Shift

Objective: Reframe distressing thoughts to gain a broader perspective and emotional balance.

Instructions:

- Write down a distressing situation. Describe the situation in detail, including who was involved, where it happened, and what occurred.

- Note your initial thoughts and feelings. Identify and write down the immediate thoughts and feelings you experienced in response to the situation.

- Challenge these thoughts by considering alternative perspectives.

- Examine your initial thoughts critically. Think about other possible explanations or viewpoints that might help you see the situation differently.

Reflection: Reflect on how this broader perspective changes your emotional response and compare your initial emotional reaction to how you feel after considering alternative viewpoints. Take note of any shifts in your feelings or thoughts, and summarize the insights gained from this exercise and how it can aid you in managing similar situations in the future.

Exercise 2: Opposite Action Practice for Emotional Transformation

Objective: Practicing opposite actions to alter unwanted emotions and promote positive behaviors.

Instructions:

- Identify an emotion you wish to change.

- Clearly describe the emotion you are experiencing and wish to alter.

- Engage in behaviors opposite to what the emotion is urging you to do.

- Actively choose behaviors that counteract the instinctual actions driven by the emotion. For instance, if you feel like isolating yourself, try to reach out to a friend.

- Implement the opposite action.

- Put the chosen opposite behaviors into practice in real-life situations where the emotion arises.

Reflection: Reflect on the impact of engaging in opposite actions. Note any changes in your emotional state and the outcomes of your actions. Summarize how this practice can assist in managing your emotions effectively.

Exercise 3: Mindfulness and Non-Judgmental Awareness

Objective: To cultivate mindfulness by staying grounded in the present moment without judgment and practicing non-judgmental awareness.

Instructions:

- **Find a Quiet Space:** Choose a quiet and comfortable place to sit undisturbed.

- **Sit Comfortably:** Sit in a comfortable position, ensuring your back is straight but not rigid.

- **Close Your Eyes and Breathe:** Gently close your eyes and take a few deep, calming breaths.

- **Observe:** Pay attention to your inner experience and surroundings without trying to change anything. Notice your thoughts, feelings, and sensations as they arise.

- **Describe:** Put words to your experiences. For instance, you might say to yourself, "I am feeling anxious," or "I notice a tingling in my hands."

- **Participate:** Engage fully in the present activity, whether it's your breath, the sounds around you, or the sensations in your body. Let go of distractions and immerse yourself in the experience.

- **Daily Practice:** Practice this exercise for five minutes daily to build a habit of mindfulness and non-judgmental awareness.

Reflection: Reflect on the experience after completing the exercise. Consider how observing, describing, and participating without judgment felt. Did it help you feel more present? What did you notice about your thoughts and sensations?

Exercise 4: Self-Compassion Letter

Objective: To practice self-compassion by expressing understanding and empathy toward oneself during times of struggle.

Instructions:

- **Identify a Recent Struggle:** Think of a recent situation where you faced a challenge or experienced emotional distress.

- **Write a Letter to Yourself:** Begin writing a letter addressed to yourself. Use kind and understanding language.

- **Express Understanding and Compassion:** In the letter, acknowledge the feelings you experienced during the struggle. Validate your emotions and recognize that it is natural to feel this way.

- **Acknowledge Your Intrinsic Worth:** Remind yourself of your intrinsic worth and strengths. Highlight positive aspects about yourself and your ability to overcome difficulties.

Reflection: Reflect on the process of writing the letter. Consider how expressing self-compassion made you feel. Did it provide a sense of relief or comfort? Note any changes in your emotional state and how this practice can assist in managing future struggles effectively.

Chapter Four

A Zeal for Life Vs Death Wish

Deathwish is a phrase that typically refers to an intense or fervent desire for death or a willingness to embrace and pursue one's demise. It can be seen as a philosophical or psychological concept, often associated with extreme ideologies, religious beliefs, or personal struggles. It's important to note that promoting or glorifying self-harm, suicide, or any form of harm to oneself or others is not healthy or encouraged.

Remove all suicidal ideation (SI) from your mind. Life is a divine gift bestowed upon us for the sacred purpose of honoring God and aiding others in their spiritual liberation. As we journey through this existence, let us embrace the vibrancy of life—the hues, vistas, melodies, flavors, and sensations that adorn our world.

The term 'zeal for death' often conveys a deep-seated yearning for the end of one's earthly journey. It is a concept with profound philosophical and spiritual connotations, sometimes linked to radical beliefs or intense personal tribulations. However, it is crucial to affirm that life is precious, and any thoughts undermining its value should be cast away.

The Gospel of Thomas offers a parable of a shepherd who, upon losing one sheep, ventures tirelessly to find it, valuing it as much as the ninety-nine that remained. This story illustrates the immeasurable worth of each individual and the lengths to which we should go to cherish and protect every life.

Every soul has meaning, and lost souls are compared to lost sheep, which are worth more when they return to the flock of our Shepherd Christ. We find this true when we read about *The Shepherd's Unyielding Love: The Parable of the Lost Sheep*.

In the Gospel, Jesus often used parables to convey profound spiritual truths. One such parable is the story of the lost sheep, which reveals God's boundless love and his unwavering concern for those who have strayed from the path.

As Jesus taught, tax collectors and sinners gathered around Him to hear His words. The Pharisees and scribes, however, criticized Him for associating with these undesirables. In response, Jesus shared the parable of the lost sheep:

> What man among you, having a hundred sheep and losing one of them, does not leave the ninety-nine in the wilderness and go after the lost one until he finds it? And when he has found it, he joyfully places it on his shoulders. Returning home, he calls together his friends and neighbors, saying, 'Rejoice with me, for I have found my lost sheep!' I tell you that in the same way, there will be more joy in heaven over one sinner who repents than over ninety-nine righteous individuals who need no repentance. (Luke 15:4-7)

The lost sheep symbolizes a sinner who has wandered away from righteousness. The shepherd represents Jesus Himself, actively seeking and rejoicing in the recovery of those who have gone astray. The heavenly joy described here underscores the significance of repentance and returning to God's fold. In the parable of the lost sheep, Jesus illustrates God's relentless pursuit of each wandering soul. Just as the shepherd actively seeks out the lost sheep, God's love knows no bounds, and He rejoices when sinners turn back to Him. The parable emphasizes that every individual matters to God. It highlights that no one is insignificant in God's eyes, and His concern extends to each of us, regardless of how lost or marginalized we may feel. The joy in heaven over a repentant sinner surpasses any other rejoicing. It underscores the transformational power of grace and forgiveness, showcasing God's boundless love and His desire for all to return to Him.

Exercises

Exercise 1: Engaging in Life's Pleasures Mindfully

Objective: Cultivate an appreciation for life's small joys and ground oneself in the present moment.

Instructions:

- **Identify Pleasures:** Make a list of activities that bring you joy and pleasure, such as walking in nature, listening to your favorite music, enjoying a good meal, or spending time with loved ones.

- **Set Intentions:** Choose one activity from your list to focus on each day. Before engaging in the activity, set an intention to fully immerse yourself in the experience.

- **Engage Fully:** During the activity, pay close attention to your senses. Notice the sights, sounds, smells, tastes, and tactile sensations. For example, if you are eating a meal, savor each bite, notice the flavors and textures, and appreciate the effort that went into preparing it.

Reflection: After the activity, take a moment to reflect on how it made you feel. Write down any positive feelings or thoughts that arose during the experience. Reflect on how these small pleasures contribute to your overall sense of well-being and appreciation for life.

Exercise 2: Building Strong Relationships

Objective: To foster meaningful connections with others, which is crucial for emotional and spiritual well-being.

Instructions:

- **Identify Key Relationships:** List the important people with whom you wish to strengthen your relationships.

- **Practice Active Listening:** When conversing with these individuals, focus on truly listening. This means putting aside distractions, making eye contact, and responding thoughtfully. Reflect back what you've heard to show that you understand and value their perspective.

- **Express Gratitude:** Regularly express your appreciation for the people in your life. This can be through verbal affirmations, written notes, or small acts of kindness.

- **Engage in Shared Activities:** Plan and engage in activities that you both enjoy. This could be anything from cooking together, taking a walk, playing a game, or participating in a mutual hobby.

- **Resolve Conflicts Gracefully:** Approach conflicts with a mindset of resolution and understanding. Practice forgiveness and strive to understand the other person's point of view, aiming to find common ground and solutions that work for both parties.

Exercise 3: Living with Intention

Objective: To lead a life aligned with your core values and purpose, fostering a sense of direction and fulfillment.

Instructions:

- **Identify Core Values:** Reflect on and write down your top five personal values. These might include honesty, compassion, creativity, faith, or family.

- **Set Intentional Goals:** Based on your values, set specific, achievable goals that align with them. For instance, if health is a core value, a goal might be to exercise three times a week or to eat more whole foods.

- **Daily Affirmations:** Start each day with a positive affirmation that aligns with your values and goals. For example, "I am committed to living a healthy and active life," or "I will approach today with compassion and understanding."

- **Reflect and Adjust:** At the end of each day, reflect on your actions and decisions. Consider how they align with your values and goals. Write down any adjustments you can make to live more intentionally.

- **Celebrate Progress:** Acknowledge and celebrate the progress you make, no matter how small. Recognize that living with intention is a continuous journey of growth and self-improvement.

These exercises can help individuals shift their focus from negative thoughts to a more positive, purposeful, and connected way of living, aligning with the theme of embracing life. In conclusion, let us affirm our commitment to life, the richness of experiences it offers, and the well-being of ourselves and those around us. Let us replace any thoughts of despair with a zeal for life, for living fully means we truly honor the divine. Let our Lord Christ shepherd your life into eternal rest; he states, "For my yolk is light."

Chapter Five

Kingdom of the Flesh

Understanding Materialism and Spiritual Wealth

In the pursuit of life, one must choose one's master wisely, for as the ancient wisdom tells us, you cannot serve both God and wealth. The quest for material riches often leads us astray from the spiritual path, binding us to a fleeting world where all is temporary.

The scripture warns, "No man can serve two masters." This phrase is a biblical quotation from the New Testament, specifically from the Gospel of Matthew in the Bible. It can be found in Matthew 6:24 (King James Version):

> No man can serve two masters, for either he will hate the one and love the other; or else he will hold to the one and despise the other. Ye cannot serve God and mammon.

In this passage, Jesus teaches about the incompatibility of serving God and wealth (represented by "mammon"). He emphasizes the idea that one's loyalty and devotion cannot be divided between two conflicting priorities. This teaching encourages a single-minded commitment to spiritual values and serving God rather than material pursuits—a profound truth from the Gospel of Matthew. It speaks to the heart of our choices, urging us to seek a higher purpose beyond the grasp of materialism.

The Apostolic Bible echoes this sentiment, advising us to store our treasures not on earth, where they are vulnerable to decay and theft, but in heaven, where they are eternal, for where your treasure lies, there too will be your heart.

Apostolic Bible:

> Treasures in [19] Treasure not to yourself treasures upon the earth! Where moth and rust obliterate, and where thieves dig through and steal. [20] But treasure up to yourself treasures in heaven! Where neither moth nor rust obliterate, and where thieves do not dig through nor steal. [21] For where [is your treasure], there will be also your heart. [22] The lamp of the body is the eye. If then your eye should be sincere, [entire body your giving light will be]. [23] But if your eye should be evil, [entire body your] will be dark. If then the light, the one in you, is darkness, [the darkness how great]? [24] No one is able [two masters to serve]; for the one he will detest, and the other love; or the one he will hold to, and the other he will disdain; you are not able to serve God and mammon.

Our world is transient, and our material possessions are impermanent. True wealth lies in the relationships we forge, rooted in faith and love—the treasures that withstand the test of time. Material possessions and worldly wealth are constantly slipping away, subject to the inexorable forces of entropy. We come into this world with nothing; ultimately, we depart with nothing. It's time to rethink the relentless pursuit of trading the precious hours of our lives for material gain. Instead, let us focus on building and nurturing profound relationships founded upon the bedrock of faith and love. These relationships are the true treasures of our existence, enduring beyond the boundaries of time and transcending the limitations of mere matter. In prioritizing meaningful connections over material possessions, we can find fulfillment and purpose that transcend the fleeting nature of material wealth.

A Lesson from *3rd Rock from the Sun*

The *3rd Rock from the Sun* is a sitcom that aired from 1996 to 2001, featuring a group of extraterrestrial beings who come to Earth and assume human identities to study the human species. The show often used aliens' misunderstandings of human culture to create comedic effects. The sitcom humorously depicts the alien Solomon family's encounter with human labor. They learn that life's truths are subjective and that the human experience is a complex tapestry of service, sacrifice, and the search for meaning beyond the daily grind. At the end of an episode, Dick concludes:

Dick Solomon: It's far more complex than I thought. There is no absolute personal truth here, and these bodies don't come with an owner's manual. Every day, these people have to make up life and truth becomes highly individual. I think these humans bend the truth because this is a difficult place to live. It's a lonely blue dot on the far end of the galaxy, and all the half-truths and flattery and diplomacy are the lubricant that people spread on each other to get over the rough spots.

In season 1, episode 15, *I Enjoy Being a Dick,* the Solomons experience working to learn about human labor. Dick, the head of the alien family, confronts Sally about her obsessive shopping habits. She decides that it's time for her and Harry to get jobs to earn their own money. However, she quickly becomes disillusioned after realizing the monotony and demands of a forty-hour work week. This episode humorously explores the aliens' reaction to and interpretations of common human experiences, in this case, the nature of work and employment. The dialogue is:

Sally: I guess I never realized how many people here are in service to others.

Dick: Well, everybody here sells his time for money. It's like taking a mortgage against your life.

Sally: My life is worth more than minimum wage and the occasional slice of free pie. I've just got to figure out what I really want to do.

Dick: I think you should. Everybody needs a goal.

The Human Condition

We all trade our time for money, but it's essential to remember that life is more than just wages. It's about finding purpose and setting goals that align with our deeper values, not just succumbing to the hedonistic treadmill of material pursuit. Consider one of the seven gifts of the holy spirit and heed Corinthians 1 12:27-30, which emphasizes that not all have the same gifts, but all are part of the body of Christ.

In conclusion, reflect upon your life's direction. Are you chasing shadows or building a legacy of love and faith? Choose your master and let your heart follow.

Exercises

Exercise 1: Setting Spiritual Goals

Objective: To set specific, measurable, achievable, relevant, and time-bound (SMART) spiritual goals.

Instructions:

- **Identify Areas for Growth:** Reflect on areas in your spiritual life where you need improvement (e.g., prayer, scripture study, service to others).

- **Set SMART Goals:** For each area, set a SMART goal. For example:
  - **Specific:** I will read the Bible for 15 minutes every morning.
  - **Measurable:** I will keep a journal to track my daily readings.
  - **Achievable:** I will start with the Gospels and then proceed to other books.
  - **Relevant:** This goal will help deepen my understanding of Christ's teachings.
  - **Time-bound:** I will achieve this goal over the next three months.

- **Plan Actions:** Outline specific actions you will take to accomplish each goal.

Reflection: At the end of each week, review your progress. Are you moving toward your goals? What adjustments do you need to make?

Exercise 2: Daily Spiritual Practice

Objective: To establish a consistent daily routine that nurtures your spiritual growth.

Instructions:

- **Morning Prayer and Meditation:** Start your day with a prayer and a few minutes of meditation on a scripture passage or a teaching of Christ.

- **Acts of Service:** Commit to performing one act of kindness daily, whether helping a neighbor, volunteering, or simply offering a kind word.

- **Evening Reflection:** End your day with a reflection on how you lived out your values and goals. Pray for guidance and strength for the following day.

Reflection: How does starting and ending your day with these practices affect your overall spiritual well-being?

Chapter Six

Foolish Wisdom vs Self

Balancing Earthly Knowledge with Spiritual Wisdom

The ancient call to 'Know thyself,' as echoed by Delphi and Socrates, and the introspective 'Cogito, ergo sum' of Descartes invite us to a deeper understanding of our essence. Consider the biblical Adam, who, upon realizing his nakedness, was asked, "Who told you that you were naked?" This narrative prompts us to reflect on our awareness and the origins of our beliefs.

Foolish or deluded wisdom of the flesh, as some might say, can distract us from true self-knowledge. Galileo Galilei's adage to 'measure what is measurable and make measurable what is not so' suggests a scientific approach to understanding the world. Yet, if we focus solely on external exploration, we risk neglecting the internal journey toward enlightenment.

The pursuit of knowledge, whether through the primordial soup theory, the intricacies of physics, or the vastness of astrology, is unending. Once familiar, the periodic table of elements now expands with new discoveries. It's a relentless quest akin to solving a million-dollar riddle or deciphering the Big Bang before returning to the earth as clay.

Socrates championed the importance of self-awareness and introspection for wisdom. Knowing your values and goals propels you forward in life. Moral injury, a profound form of PTSD, arises when actions conflict with deeply held values. Whether innate or shaped by experience, these values guide our reactions and interactions.

Dr. Prem Jagyasi, a renowned global leader and life coach, emphasizes that our values, whether recognized or not, steer our lives. His experiences across cultures underscore the universality of this principle.

For example, imagine twin brothers raised identically but with one critical difference: their core values. Brother A values money above all, while Brother B cherishes family. Both work the same blue-collar job, clocking in forty hours a week, barely scraping above the poverty line, devoid of simple pleasures.

Driven by their desires, they extend their work week to sixty hours to afford the latest iPhone. This decision comes at a cost—their family's time with a father, a husband. The family feels the absence deeply, yet the brothers' responses diverge.

Brother A, motivated by his value of providing financially, endures the extra hours without emotional turmoil, believing he's enhancing their lifestyle. In contrast, Brother B, who holds family time sacred, experiences significant distress, finding the extended hours increasingly unbearable.

This tale illustrates the profound impact of our values on our well-being.

Identifying and understanding your values—perhaps selecting the top five that resonate with you and committing them to memory—can shield you from moral conflict and guide you through life's challenging decisions without the shadow of mental distress.

By aligning your actions with your values, you navigate life with integrity and foresight, avoiding the pitfalls of moral injury and the mental anguish that comes from living in contradiction to what you hold dear. It's not just about knowing your values; it's about living them.

In another example, if you value respect and your spouse disrespects you, this may trigger you and cause you to react in a way that may violate some of your other values, such as protection or family. Do you truly know yourself—your goals, values, and triggers? Understanding these aspects of your identity is crucial for living authentically and avoiding the pitfalls of fleshly knowledge.

Delphi, the ancient Greek sanctuary, was home to the Oracle of Delphi, where divine wisdom was sought. At the entrance to the Temple of Apollo, the famous inscription 'know thyself' (pronounced gnothi seauton) greeted visitors. This powerful phrase, attributed to various ancient Greek sages, is one of the Delphic maxims. It underscores the critical importance of self-awareness and introspection. By understanding your nature, limitations, and place in the world, you take the first step toward knowing thyself, laying the groundwork for personal growth, ethical living, and true wisdom.

Before mastering the art of self-fulfillment, it's crucial to unearth your core values. These values silently steer the course of your life, whether you acknowledge them or not. In this initial exercise, select five values that you consider indispensable. Picture this: if you were alone and faced with a life-or-death situation, forced to declare your five values, what would they be? Or picture yourself as the head of a household, your children seeking guidance on values. Pinpointing these fundamental values marks the primary stride toward self-awareness, paving the way for personal development, principled living, and profound understanding.

Personal Growth and Self-Development

In this exercise, take a fluorescent highlighter and highlight five values from the list:

Achievement	Honesty	Patience
Adaptability	Hope	Perseverance
Autonomy	Humility	Self-control
Balance	Imagination	Self-discipline
Confidence	Independence	Success
Courage	Inner Peace	Vitality
Decisiveness	Integrity	Willpower
Determination	Knowledge	Wisdom
Fortitude	Learning	Zeal
Grit	Logic	Zest
Growth	Love of Learning	
Health	Meaningful Work	

Relationships and Social Connection

Community	Inclusivity	Respect for Others
Connection	Love	Support
Empathy	Marriage	Teamwork
Family	Partnership	Trust
Friendship	Respect	Understanding

Emotional and Mental Well-being

Authenticity	Gratitude	Open-mindedness
Cheerfulness	Humor	Peace
Compassion	Modesty	Playfulness
Forgiveness	Openness	Thankfulness

Adventure and Exploration

Adventure	Ethics and Values	Morality
Boldness	Benevolence	Righteousness
Challenge	Environmental Stewardship	Sacrifice
Creativity		Service
Fun	Faith	Spirituality
Innovation	Generosity	Stewardship
Risk-taking	Justice	Tolerance
Spontaneity	Kindness	Truth

Professional and Social Status

Fame	Productivity	Stability
Influence	Prosperity	Wealth
Leadership	Recognition	
Power	Security	

Understanding our values is like understanding the number values on the bevel of a compass. We need to understand not only the way the metaphorical needle points us in our azimuth toward life but also how it aligns with our values. Are we navigating away from or toward what we stand for?

Lastly, this is a spiritual guide, so an excerpt in prayer is warranted. When we pray, we pray with fervor. It is believed that St. Thomas Aquinas would dance and praise the lord with poetry and positive energy. It is in our nature to use specific speech patterns, whether we are engaging Wernicke's speech center in thought or using auditory tensioning and vocal cords while using Broca's speech center to gently pacify and coo a baby or speak gently to a loved one. Patterns in speech and thought are equally important to the word's content summoned. We wouldn't want to express gratitude halfheartedly to our loved ones in the flesh, so why would we consider doing the same with God spiritually?

Chapter Seven

The Virtue of Forgiveness and the Consequences of Vengeance

In the face of adversity, embrace the wisdom of restraint. Extend forgiveness, for often, the transgressions of others stem from ignorance. Forgiveness is not just an act of mercy toward others but a gift to oneself. Clinging to anger and resentment is akin to consuming poison while hoping the other suffers. Instead, establish boundaries to heal relationships or find peace in letting go. True strength lies not in vengeance but in forgiveness. It is this power that can move mountains and transform hearts.

Mary imparts the Savior's teachings on achieving inner stability and divine rest. She reveals that our true adversaries are not just external but also lie within, manifesting as darkness, desire, ignorance, and wrath. It is through recognizing and overcoming these internal battles that we find true freedom.

Proverbs 12:5:

> The thoughts of the just are righteous, while the schemes of the wicked are deceitful.

It is through discerning wisdom that we navigate life's complexities. The intentions of the vengeful are misguided, while the actions of the righteous seek healing. It is through prudent reflection that we avoid the pitfalls of revenge.

The Gospel of Thomas:

> The one who unravels the meaning behind these teachings will transcend the confines of mortality, embracing the fullness of life. Let us seek understanding and live in the light of truth, for it is there that we find our salvation from death's grasp. The one who misinterprets these teachings may fall into the abyss of bitterness, never escaping the shadows of death. Let us pursue clarity and dwell in the realm of forgiveness, for it is there that we find our liberation from the chains of vengeance.

In the shadow of conflict, resist the impulse for retribution. Reject vengeance, for it often escalates the cycle of harm and perpetuates ignorance. Vengeance is not an act of justice but a path to further discord. Holding onto anger and seeking retribution is like igniting a fire within oneself, expecting the other to burn. Instead, pursue resolution to mend relationships or find closure in moving forward.

The Weakness of Vengeance

True weakness is found in the pursuit of vengeance. It is a power that can shatter lives and harden hearts.

These consequences challenge the soul's integrity, questioning its moral compass. Yet, the soul, entangled in earthly vendettas, risks being consumed by darkness, having succumbed to the chains of spite and malice. It speaks of entrapment in a world of turmoil, longing for peace that remains elusive.

The Path to Inner Turmoil

Our true adversaries are not only external but also internal, manifesting as anger, envy, malice, and vengeance. By acknowledging and resisting these internal conflicts, we can avoid the snares of retribution.

Ephesians 4:31-32 calls us to cast aside bitterness, wrath, and anger, urging us to be kind, compassionate, and forgiving, just as Christ has forgiven us.

Resentment and anger are challenging emotions to navigate. Yet, Romans 10:13 promises salvation to all who call upon the Lord's name.

Peter 1:18-19 reflects on redemption, not through perishable items like silver or gold, but through the precious blood of Christ. Before Christ, sacrifices were made annually for our sins. Christ's crucifixion, the ultimate sacrifice of an unblemished lamb, means that all our sins are forgiven. The tearing of the temple curtain at the moment of His death symbolizes the end of such offerings, releasing the Holy Spirit and completing the Holy Trinity.

Therefore, forgive yourself, for through Christ's sacrifice, God has already granted you forgiveness

Exercises

Exercise 1: Forgiveness and Emotional Release

Objective: To release unresolved judgments and grudges that lead to physiological stress and to cultivate forgiveness as a gift to oneself, independent of reconciliation with others.

Instructions:

- **Identify Someone to Forgive:** Reflect on someone you need to forgive. This could be someone who has wronged you or caused you emotional pain.

- **Write a Letter:** Write a letter to this person, expressing your feelings and your decision to let go of the resentment. This letter is for your eyes only and will not be sent.

- **Prayer and Meditation:** Engage in daily prayer or meditation to find solace and clarity. This helps reinforce your decision to forgive and promotes emotional healing.

Exercise 2: Guided Meditation on Forgiveness

Instructions:

- **Find a Comfortable Place to Sit:** Choose a quiet and comfortable place to sit undisturbed.

- **Close Your Eyes and Breathe:** Gently close your eyes and take a few deep, calming breaths.

- **Visualize:** Visualize the person you need to forgive. Picture them in your mind as clearly as possible.

- **Mentally Repeat:** Mentally repeat the phrase, "I forgive you, and I release this burden." Allow yourself to feel the emotions that arise.

- **Continue for Several Minutes:** Continue this meditation for several minutes, feeling the weight lift from your heart with each repetition.

Reflection: Reflect on the experience after completing the exercise. Consider how expressing your feelings and practicing forgiveness made you feel. Did you notice a sense of relief or lightness?

Daily Practice: Incorporate this guided meditation into your daily routine to build a habit of forgiveness and emotional release.

Exercise 3: Forgiveness and Reconciliation

Objective: To practice forgiveness as taught by Christ, enhancing spiritual peace and relationships.

Instructions:

- **Scripture Reading:** Read Matthew 18:21-22 and reflect on Christ's teaching about forgiveness.

- **Identify Hurts:** Write down any grudges or unresolved conflicts you have.

- **Prayer for Healing:** Pray for the strength to forgive and ask God to help you let go of any bitterness.

- **Act of Reconciliation:** Reach out to someone you need to forgive or seek forgiveness from. This can be through a conversation, a letter, or a symbolic act of letting go.

Reflection: How does practicing forgiveness change your relationships and your spiritual state? What new insights do you gain from this process?

Conclusion: In this chapter, we have explored the impact of judgment and ignorance on our well-being. By practicing open-minded thinking, mindfulness, self-compassion, and forgiveness, we can overcome these obstacles and move toward a life of greater peace and understanding. Remember, our journey toward self-improvement is ongoing, and each step forward is a victory.

Chapter Eight

Christ Did Not Taste Death

Webster's Dictionary: 2. A sin-offering; an offering made to atone for sin.

He hath made him to be sin for us, who knew no sin. 2 Cor. v.

Now let us visit Second Corinthians Chapter 5, verse 21:

> [21] God made him who had no sin to be sin for us, so that in him we might become the righteousness of God.

The crucifixion of Christ the Redeemer Jesus accepted his fate with dignity and honor, as prophesied by Isaiah. The prophet Isaiah addressed the kingdom of Judah for forty years, beginning in the year that King Uzziah died (around 740 BC) and continuing at least until the Assyrian siege of Jerusalem in 701 BC. He provided godly counsel to Kings Ahaz and Hezekiah when the powerful Assyrian Empire threatened the nation. Isaiah maintained an international perspective, understanding that events, challenges, and opportunities are interconnected on a global scale. He recognized the interplay between nations, regions, and individuals in a rapidly changing world, revealing that Israel's life was bound up with the affairs of the broader world. Isaiah urged care for the poor and needy, commitment to follow God's ways and pursuit of social and economic justice.

About 700 years before Christ came, the prophet Isaiah 53:3-8 depicts the suffering of the Messiah:

> **Isaiah 53:3:** But his appearance was without honor, and wanting by sons of men. A man for calamity, knowing how to bear infirmity. For he turned his face; he was dishonored and not considered.
> **Isaiah 53:4:** This one bore our sins, and on account of us, he was grieved. We considered him stricken, smitten by God, and afflicted.
> **Isaiah 53:5:** But he was wounded for our transgressions, bruised for our iniquities. The punishment for our peace was upon him, and by his stripes, we are healed.
> **Isaiah 53:6:** All we like sheep have gone astray; we have turned, everyone, to his own way. And the Lord has laid on him the iniquity of us all.
> **Isaiah 53:7:** He was oppressed and afflicted, yet he opened not his mouth. He was led like a lamb to the slaughter, and as a sheep before its shearers is silent, so he did not open his mouth.
> **Isaiah 53:8:** By oppression and judgment, he was taken away. And who can speak of his descendants? For he was cut off from the land of the living; for the transgression of my people, he was stricken.

Mark 15:15 narrates Pilate's role, "Wanting to satisfy the crowd, Pilate released Barabbas to them. He had Jesus flogged and handed him over to be crucified."

Jesus' first punishment was by the governor's troops, "Pilate ordered Jesus flogged with a lead-tipped whip."

They lacerated his torso and legs with a cat-o'-nine-tails thirty-nine times (2 Corinthians 11:24). It was believed that forty lashes would kill a man, so thirty-nine were given. The metal shards at the tips of the nine leather straps would bruise and lacerate the victim's flesh when applied and rip holes in the tissue when removed. Rome often used this painful torture to deter crimes against the state, but in Jesus' case, it only accelerated his death.

The Romans offered Jesus cheap vinegar wine, which had a drug mixed in to dull the senses. It was the custom of the Romans to provide a man being crucified drugged wine so that he might more easily endure his cross. Jesus refused the wine, however, apparently so that He could go through his suffering with a clear mind.

The passion of Christ involved unimaginable suffering. Jesus' body became adorned with numerous open wounds after the scourging, subjecting Him to acute agony. The intensity of this pain, coupled with the loss of blood, drained His energy, making even the simple act of moving monumental. Soldiers mockingly placed a purple cloth on His wounded back, accentuating His pain (Mark 15:17). Additionally, Jesus bore the weight of the crown of thorns.

The representation of Jesus carrying the cross has evolved over centuries. While many depictions show Him carrying the entire cross, historical considerations suggest that the vertical part of the cross may have been permanently positioned in the ground. Golgotha, also known as Calvary (Matthew 27:33), served as Jerusalem's designated site for crucifixions. The condemned would carry the crossbeam from the prison to the crucifixion site. The crossbeam, weighing approximately 100 pounds, presented a daunting challenge for anyone, let alone Jesus, who had endured a night in prison, brutal scourging, and condemnation by His own people. Jesus stumbled and fell three times under the weight of the crossbeam, unable to break His fall each time due to His arms being bound. Soldiers enlisted Simon of Cyrene to assist Him (Luke 23:26).

Upon reaching Calvary, Jesus endured the indignity of being stripped of His garments. Roman crucifixion aimed to inflict the most gruesome and degrading death possible, stripping the condemned naked. Iron spikes, five to seven inches long, were driven through the wrists of the condemned into the crossbeam, and the feet were nailed to the vertical beam.

Death by crucifixion resulted from a combination of severe blood loss from scourging and asphyxiation caused by the constrained position. The crucified individual's ability to breathe was hindered, forcing shallow breaths until their strength dwindled. To gasp for air, they had to painfully push their body up with their feet, exacerbating their suffering. The wounds in their hands and feet were subjected to further pressure, and their lacerated back scraped against the rough wooden beam. Death ensued due to the gradual weakening of the intercostal muscles and diaphragm, leading to asphyxiation.

These details paint a vivid picture of the unimaginable agony endured by those sentenced to crucifixion, underscoring the severity of this punishment. Jesus, while enduring this agony, uttered seven last words from the cross, each with great effort and difficulty. The executioners ensured the demise of the crucified individuals by breaking their legs with a heavy mallet or thrusting a spear through their torso. While Jesus was spared the former, He was not spared the latter, even though He had already passed away (John 19:31-37).

Recorded History

Quintilian, the renowned Latin teacher and writer (AD 35-96), highlighted the brutal nature of crucifixion in his work Declamationes 6.9. His influence extends beyond teaching and writing, contributing significantly to historical understanding today.

By understanding the physical suffering Jesus endured during the crucifixion, we gain a deeper appreciation of His sacrifice.

Cicero, the Roman statesman and philosopher, expressed his aversion to crucifixion, deeming it horrific. He suggested that the word *cross* should be entirely avoided in polite society, illustrating the profound and vile nature of crucifixion.

"Let the very word 'cross' be far removed from not only the bodies of Roman citizens but even from their thoughts, their eyes, and their ears." Cicero, 106-43 BC, Pro Rabirio Postumo.

Chapter Nine

The Fate of the Apostles and Their Divine Mission

The Apostles' story is one of profound faith, extraordinary courage, and unwavering dedication. These men, chosen by Jesus Christ himself, spread the word of God and established the foundations of Christianity. Each apostle's journey, marked by their teachings and often brutal martyrdom, is a testament to their commitment to the divine mission.

These men carried the torch to all parts of the earth after the resurrection of Jesus so that one day, His teachings would reach you—if you so choose to be an ear of the great news. Like the concept of *free will*, this is not for everyone, and unfortunately, the sacrifices of our Lord Christ and the Apostles who carried his message will fall on deaf ears. Though for those who spread the great news and rally those to preach the great news, they will aid in strengthening each other's faith. As the saying goes, "Iron sharpens iron."

In fact, for the first 300 years, Christians used symbols such as the Chi-Ro and fish symbol to silently express to other Christians that they were not pagans and followers of Christ our Lord. This is a strong visual of bona fides, where, in these times, such an offense to the Roman Republic could lead to an excruciating, painful death. It wasn't until the emperor Constantine blended both the Christian faith and Roman Paganism into what is officially called Roman Catholicism. However, certain elements were included to accommodate both faiths into one. We encourage you to seek, find, and juxtapose what these early differences could mean.

Simon Peter: The Rock of the Church Peter, originally a fisherman named Simon, was renamed by Jesus to Peter, meaning "rock." He was imprisoned and flogged for his faith (Acts 4:3; 5:18, 40). Tradition holds that Peter was martyred in Rome during Emperor Nero's reign, crucified upside down. His legacy includes the letters 1 and 2 Peter, which continue to inspire believers.

Andrew: The Saint of the X-Shaped Cross Andrew, Peter's brother and a fisherman was known for his unwavering devotion to spreading the gospel. He met a martyr's fate, reportedly being crucified on an X-shaped cross in Patras, Greece. After being whipped severely by seven soldiers they tied his body to the cross with cords to prolong his agony. His followers reported that, when he was led toward the cross, Andrew saluted it in these words, "I have long desired and expected this happy hour. The cross has been consecrated by the body of Christ hanging on it". He continued to preach to his tormentors for two days until he expired. The X-shaped cross is now recognized as Saint Andrew's Cross. His ultimate sacrifice symbolizes his steadfast commitment to his faith, inspiring many with his exemplary dedication.

James, Son of Zebedee: The First Martyr James, the son of Zebedee, holds the title of the first apostle to be martyred. His unwavering faith led to his tragic beheading by the order of King Herod Agrippa I around 44 AD (Acts 12:1-2). As a strong leader of the church, James was beheaded at Jerusalem. The Roman officer who guarded James watched amazed as James defended his faith at his trial. Later, the officer Walked beside James to the place of execution. Overcome by conviction, he declared his new faith to the judge and knelt beside James to accept beheading as a Christian. His courageous sacrifice marked the beginning of the apostles' enduring commitment to their beliefs.

John: The Apostle of Love and Revelation John, brother of James, stands out among the apostles for his unique fate. Despite surviving being boiled in oil during a wave of persecution In Rome and forced to drink poison, he was exiled to the mines in the prison island of Patmos, where he received the divine vision that became the Book of Revelation. The apostle John was later freed and returned to serve As Bishop of Edessa in modern Turkey. He died as an old man, the only apostle to die peacefully. His enduring legacy includes the Gospel of John and three epistles, all emphasizing love and faith.

Mark: Died in Alexandria, Egypt, after being dragged by Horses through the streets until he was dead.

Philip: Martyred in Phrygia Philip's unyielding faith led to his martyrdom in Hierapolis, Phrygia, where he was crucified upside down according to tradition. His steadfastness in the face of adversity is commemorated in the lost Gospel of Philip, leaving a lasting testament to his unshakable devotion.

Bartholomew: Flayed and Crucified Bartholomew, also known as Nathanael, faced a gruesome end. He was a missionary to Asia. He witnessed for our Lord in present day Turkey. Bartholomew was martyred for his preaching in Armenia where he was flayed flayed alive in Albanopolis (Urbanopolis). His harrowing fate serves as a poignant reminder of the severe persecutions endured by the apostles for their unwavering dedication to their beliefs.

Matthew: The Evangelist to Ethiopia Matthew, once a tax collector, met his martyrdom in Ethiopia, reportedly killed by a king who opposed his preaching and the conversion of the king's daughter. Suffered martyrdom in Ethiopia,

Killed by a sword wound. His Gospel portrays Jesus as fulfilling God's promises to Israel, leaving a lasting impact on the Christian faith.

Thomas: The Doubter Turned Martyr Thomas, often remembered for his initial doubt, ultimately displayed unwavering faith. He met his martyrdom in India, reportedly being stabbed to death during one of his missionary trips to establish the church in the Subcontinent. His resounding declaration, "My Lord and my God," serves as a testament to his unyielding devotion to Jesus Christ.

Matthias: Chosen to Replace Judas Matthias, fearlessly preached in Judea and Ethiopia. Tradition holds that he met his end through stoning and then beheading with an axe in Colchis at the hands of the many pagans there, unwaveringly spreading the gospel until the very end.

Paul (Saul): The Greatest Missionary Paul, formerly a persecutor of Christians, underwent a transformative vision, becoming the most influential apostle. Paul endured numerous hardships, including beatings, shipwrecks, and a lengthy imprisonment, but remained steadfast in his mission. During his imprisonment, he wrote many epistles to the churches he had established across the Roman Empire, teaching foundational Christian doctrines. These letters form a substantial part of the New Testament, leaving an enduring impact on Christianity. Ultimately, Paul was tortured and beheaded by Emperor Nero in Rome in A.D. 67

Jude and Simon: Met martyrdom alongside in Beirut. Tradition holds that they were either hacked to death, beheaded, or killed with arrows when they refused to deny their faith in Christ leaving an enduring legacy of unwavering faith.

Luke: The Beloved Physician Luke, the beloved physician and author of the Gospel of Luke and Acts, is believed to have died in Greece. He was hanged in Greece as a result of his tremendous Preaching to the lost. His detailed accounts of Jesus' life and the early church continue to provide invaluable insight into the

Christian faith.

The unwavering dedication of the apostles in spreading the message of Jesus Christ serves as a testament to their profound commitment. Their sacrifices have left an indelible mark on the history of Christianity, inspiring and fortifying the faith of believers worldwide. How can we quantify the profound sacrifices made for contemporary humanity to have the fundamental freedom to practice religion?

Conclusion

Embracing Spiritual Growth

The journey of spiritual growth is illuminated by the wisdom of biblical teachings and the insights shared herein. Key lessons emphasize the importance of morning gratitude rituals, transforming thoughts into positive behavior, and aligning actions with core values. These exercises encourage individuals to cultivate a pure heart and mind, promoting inner peace and spiritual well-being. Individuals can embark on a transformative journey toward spiritual growth by understanding the concept of darkness in spiritual growth and actively working to replace negative thoughts with positive actions.

Overcoming Ignorance and Embracing Knowledge

The text emphasizes the significance of overcoming ignorance and embracing knowledge as essential components of spiritual development. Individuals are encouraged to cultivate open-minded thinking and self-compassion through mindfulness and non-judgmental awareness.

Reflective journaling and the exploration of personal growth and self-development serve as practical tools for individuals to gain clarity and insight, fostering a deeper understanding of their spiritual journey. By recognizing the impact of ignorance and actively seeking knowledge, individuals can navigate a path of enlightenment and personal growth.

The Power of Forgiveness and Letting Go

The virtue of forgiveness and the transformative power of letting go are highlighted as crucial elements of spiritual evolution. Practical exercises, including guided meditation on forgiveness and writing a forgiveness letter, provide individuals with actionable steps to release anger and resentment. By engaging in practices of forgiveness, prayer, and meditation for healing, individuals can experience emotional liberation and spiritual renewal. Embracing the virtue of forgiveness enables individuals to transcend past grievances, fostering inner peace and spiritual growth.

These powers question the soul's journey, challenging its very essence. Yet, the soul, unbound by earthly ties, responds with enlightenment, having overcome the shackles of desire and ignorance. It speaks of liberation from a transient world, finding solace in eternal silence.

Baptism & Encouragement for Ongoing Spiritual Growth

To be a follower of Christ, one must embrace the belief that Jesus died to atone for all sins with a single selfless act. During a typical baptism, a public declaration is made as water is poured over the individual's forehead.

The officiant asks, **"Do you accept that our Lord Jesus Christ came and died for our sins?"**

To which the response is, **"Yes."**

Subsequently, the person is baptized **in the name of the Father, the Son, and the Holy Spirit.**

This act serves as a public declaration, signifying one's understanding and acceptance of Jesus as the unblemished lamb and the ultimate blood sacrifice, embodying God's only perfect son. By partaking in this public declaration, a person openly professes their comprehension and embrace of the belief that Yahweh incarnated as Jesus and lived a flawless life. This acknowledgment emphasizes Jesus' sacrificial role in absolving humanity's sins, thereby solidifying one's commitment to follow in his footsteps. In essence, becoming a follower of Christ involves a profound acceptance of Jesus' pivotal role as the perfect sacrifice for the salvation of humanity. Through baptism and the public declaration it entails, individuals publicly acknowledge their belief in Jesus' redemptive sacrifice and express their commitment to live according to His teachings.

Final Blessing and Call to Action

The great commission involves spreading the gospel in scripture, spreading the gospel, or "the great news," as it is commonly referred to today. The Bible encourages us to relish this information but also share it with the world. Matthew 12:30, where Jesus says, "He who is not with me is against me, and he who does not gather with me scatters." This verse underscores the necessity of a clear stance in one's faith and allegiance. We demonstrate this to God when we spread His w ord.

Merriam-Webster defines the gospel as:

Gos'pel, n. [Sax. *Godspell*; *god*, good, and *spell*, history, relation, narration, word, speech, that which is uttered, announced, sent, or communicated; answering to the history of the birth, life, actions, death, resurrection, ascension and doctrines of Jesus Christ; or a revelation of the grace of God to fallen man through a mediator, including the character, actions, and doctrines of Christ, which whole scheme of salvation, as revealed by Christ and his apostles. This gospel is said to have been preached to Abraham by the promise, "In thee shall all nations be blessed." Gal. Iii. 8.

It is called the gospel of God. Rom.i.1. It is called the gospel of Christ. Rom.1.16 It is called the gospel of salvation. Eph.i.13.

God's word.

Divinity; theology.

We can use the information in this guide to lead others into salvation by baptizing nations in the name of the Father, the Son, and the Holy Spirit.

Author's Note

The belief in Christ as our redeemer purchases us eternal salvation. It is common for those even in the closest circles of Jesus to doubt. Take the story of doubting Thomas, for instance; he had to witness the resurrection and wounds on Jesus to fully convince him that he is our savior. "Thomas's Doubt and the Blessing of Faith"

In the Gospel of John, we encounter the story of Thomas, one of the twelve disciples. Thomas was absent when Jesus appeared to the other disciples after His resurrection. Upon hearing their testimony, Thomas expressed skepticism, declaring that he would only believe if he could physically see and touch the wounds in Jesus' hands and side.

Jesus, in His infinite compassion, did not rebuke Thomas for his doubt. Instead, He appeared to Thomas eight days later, even though the doors were locked.

Standing in their midst, Jesus greeted them with the words, "Peace to you." He then turned His attention to Thomas, inviting him to examine His hands and side.

"Bring your finger here," Jesus said, "and behold my hands; bring your hand and put it into my side. Be not unbelieving, but believing!"

Thomas' response was profound: "My Lord and my God."

In that moment, he moved from doubt to unwavering faith. Jesus' reply to Thomas carries a timeless message: "Because you have seen me, you have believed; blessed are those who have not seen and yet have believed." This statement extends the blessings of faith to all future believers— those who, like us, won't physically encounter Jesus but will trust in Him through faith.

The passage continues, emphasizing the purpose of recording these events and writings. It clarifies that they intend to strengthen readers' faith, enabling them to believe that Jesus is the Christ, the Son of God. Through this belief, they attain the promise of eternal life.

In essence, this passage underscores the significance of having faith in Jesus Christ as the Son of God and the Savior, even in the absence of direct physical evidence. It encourages believers to place their trust in Jesus and His sacrificial atonement for the forgiveness of sins. Faith brings the blessings of salvation and eternal life—a message that resonates across generations and can be shared with believers and non-believers alike.

Appendix

Additional Resources for Spiritual Growth

Reading the book of Matthew is a great way to visit the teachings of Christ in chronological order. Encourage others to join you in a Bible study and discuss the significance of these deep meanings.

Prayers and Meditations

The Lord's Prayer, also known as the "Our Father," is a powerful and essential prayer in Christianity, widely recited across different denominations. It is a foundational prayer in the New Testament, appearing in Matthew (6:9-13) and Luke (11:2-4). The King James Version (KJV) presents the following rendition of the prayer:

> Our Father which art in heaven, Hallowed be thy name. Thy kingdom come, thy will be done in earth, as it is in heaven. Give us this day our daily bread. And forgive us our debts as we forgive our debtors. And lead us not into temptation but deliver us from evil. For thine is the kingdom, and the power, and the glory, forever. A men.

This prayer serves as a powerful model for Christian prayer, emphasizing the reverence for God, the coming of God's kingdom, provision for daily needs, forgiveness, guidance, and deliverance from evil.

Immerse yourself in a transformative morning routine with the *Morning Gratitude Ritual*. This powerful practice involves dedicating five minutes daily to breathe deeply and reflect on three things you are grateful for. This simple yet impactful exercise sets the tone for a positive and fulfilling day ahead.

Furthermore, embrace the concept of *Non-Judgmental Awareness* by devoting five minutes daily to mindfulness, fostering a habit of non-judgmental awareness. This practice sets the stage for a more peaceful and centered mindset.

Experience the profound effects of self-care with the *Self-Compassion Letter* exercise, which entails writing a compassionate letter to yourself to acknowledge and understand recent struggles. Spending ten to fifteen minutes on this exercise can be incredibly healing and uplifting.

Moreover, integrate spirituality into your daily routine with the *Daily Spiritual Practice* section. Begin your day with *Morning Prayer and Meditation*, dedicating five to ten minutes to prayer and meditation on a scripture passage or teaching. Additionally, the *Gratitude Journal* prompts you to jot down three things you are grateful for each day, fostering a positive outlook. Incorporate acts of kindness into your routine with *Acts of Service*, varying in time but consistently spreading positivity and compassion.

Conclude your day with *Evening Reflection* and *Reflective Journaling*, spending five to ten minutes on each to introspect on your values and personal growth.

Lastly, dedicate ten minutes to *Mindfulness Meditation* each day, focusing on your breath and observing your thoughts without judgment. By combining these practices, you can allocate thirty to forty-five minutes daily, adjusting the time based on your personal pace and depth of engagement with each exercise. Embrace this holistic approach to self-care and personal growth and experience the profound impact of a daily gratitude and mindfulness routine.